RICHARD ROWE

PROPHECY *versus* DISCERNMENT

Cover Design by O.Y.R. Books and Publishing

ISBN: 9798355041724 (Paperback)

Dedication

With sincere gratitude, I dedicate this book to my mother, Donna Smith, my father, Richard Rowe, and my uncle Robert Rowe. Your support along the varying terrains of my spiritual journey will always hold a special place in my heart. Thank you for being among the sounding boards of wisdom and offering guidance as I start a new chapter—a new book.

Content

Foreword...7

Introduction..10

Chapter 1 12

Confusion in "Thus Saith the Lord" 12

Chapter 2 23

Did God say that? 23

Chapter 3 26

Seven Sources of Prophecy.................................26

Chapter 4 46

Prophecy as a Gift..46

Chapter 5 52

The Gift of Discernment......................................52

Chapter 6 61

When the Gifts Clashes 61

Chapter 7 67

Intercession..67

Chapter 8 74

Tools for Intercession 74

Conclusion 78

Foreword

I had the great fortune of meeting Prophet Richard Rowe on several occasions. We share a good spiritual father-son relationship. Words escape me as I try to describe how amazing the author of this book is.

I am deeply moved by his unconditional love and compassion for the things of God. It is heartwarming to see how people are drawn to God by his humility in Christ Jesus. I am very proud of him and his growth as a young man who stands out from those in ministry who have not had that heart for the work of God.

If asked, Prophet Rowe would say that he cannot do what he does all by himself but through the grace of God on his side. I want to thank God for giving Prophet Rowe such insight and love for His people. Over the years, I have found him to be a man who loves God and God's people. He has been humble and faithful to the Lord, his family, and the church.

I have watched him grow favorably in the Word of God, gaining spiritual strength and insight to continue his journey with the King. He has increased in the revelation knowledge of God's word, faith, the prophetic, miracles, deliverance, and signs and wonders which follow his ministry. Prophet Rowe does not compromise; he does not settle for mediocrity.

He has never been afraid to administer the truth of God. He is solid, rooted, and grounded in his faith. He is a role model for many, especially the younger generation, who emulate him as a mentor and spiritual leader. Without a doubt, God is with him, and He is using him for His glory.

Prophecy versus Discernment is Prophet Rowe's first book, yet this is one of the most inspirational, insightful revelations I have ever read. I have never seen anyone write a book so precisely on the prophetic versus discernment as he has so masterfully done. When I read this book, I'm transported to a classroom where a professor of theology is lecturing soundly. This is the kind of book you cannot ignore. It is a must-read.

I have read the manuscript about four times, and I was blown away by the knowledge it contains, which, I believe, came from the depth of the spirit of Christ. Congratulations on your successful book journey, Prophet Rowe. May God bless you endlessly. I am so proud of you and will always be, but God is even prouder. *"Keep on keeping on"* for the name of Jesus Christ. May you be a blessing to the nations of the earth. May God spread your wings both near and far, and may you never lack anything you aim to achieve in Jesus' name. To all of Prophet Richard Rowe's amazing supporters, I urge you to read this book and spread this message to everyone until it reaches the four corners of the earth.

- Bishop R.A. McKenzie

Introduction

Prophecy vs. Discernment is a book that will open the eyes of readers to solid and basic information about the prophetic. Too often, personalities that create an illusion for entertainment are associated with the prophetic; but we should never forget the foundational biblical guide that keeps us in line.

In this book lies the answer to silent questions and concerns of prophetic people, and it will help bring clarity to the differences between the gift of prophecy and the gift of discernment.

The book will also underscore their respective functions in the Body of Christ and enlighten readers about the sources of prophecy. This book was birthed from a direct command from the Lord to write. Inspiration also came from experiences in the low seasons in my life.

I later discovered that some of the most significant personal advancements occur during one's lowest seasons. Nelson Mandela was arrested on several occasions and stood trial four times. He spent over 27 years in prison before becoming South Africa's president. Paul the Apostle was incarcerated when he wrote four letters (Ephesians, Philippians, Colossians, and Philemon) which form part of the New Testament in the bible. As a word of encouragement, remember that your experience of a down season does not mean you are defeated; it may be the Lord's way of birthing something great in you for nations. I am honored that the Lord chose me to release this information to His people.

Chapter 1

Confusion in "Thus Saith the Lord"

Often as believers, we may not be insightful or well educated on the realms of the Spirit and, therefore, not exposed to advanced spiritual matters. As a result, it is harder to discern or detect what is directly from the Lord, the heart, mind, or an unknown source. Many have misrepresented our Lord Jesus Christ by using his name to push a hidden agenda, which has caused many to turn their backs on prophecies and prophetic vessels. There are still many who walked away after receiving a prophetic word with questions or statements like:

- Was that the Lord speaking?
- I don't think they are hearing from God.
- God didn't tell me that!
- That's a false prophet! (*Our favorite line*)
- That came from the wrong vein!

1 Thessalonians 5:20-21 (AMPC)

Do not spurn the gifts and utterances of the prophets [do not depreciate prophetic revelations nor despise inspired instruction or exhortation or warning]

[20] But test and prove all things [until you can recognize] what is good; [to that] holdfast.

While there is nothing wrong with questioning the source of a prophecy, we must not miss out on what is of God by misjudging, overthinking, and *'under comprehending'* what was said by a prophetic vessel.

For example, Naaman, the commander of the Army of the King of Syria, would have missed out on his healing because he *almost* disobeyed the prophetic instruction from Elisha, the Prophet. This was because the *word* did not suit his ego. Thanks to the servants who told him to follow the Prophet's instruction to receive his divine healing. See 2 Kings 5:1-19.

Another example of a man who ignored instructions given in a prophecy from God through a prophetic vessel, costing him his life, can be found in *1 Kings 20*.

Prophecy vs Discernment

1 Kings chapter 20:35-36 reads:

35 *And a certain man of the sons of the prophets said unto his neighbor in the word of the LORD, smite me, I pray thee. And the man refused to smite him.*

36 *Then said he unto him, because thou hast not obeyed the voice of the LORD, behold, as soon as thou art departed from me, a lion shall slay thee. And as soon as he was departed from him, a lion found him and slew him.*

One Thursday night, I was praying and imparting into the lives of three other prophets. They invited a lady on the line that needed prayer, and while praying for her, the Lord told me there was an evil plot against her in the spiritual realm. The Lord revealed that this plot could be broken, but only if she surrendered her life to him. I told her, *"I see an evil plot against your life in the spirit. The enemy wants to take your life by September 16, but the Lord said if you give him your life, it will not prevail."* She responded that her church had already offered up prayers on her behalf and prayer warriors there suggested that she would be fine.

The instruction was for her to surrender her life to God; however, she chose to ignore the instruction. Around the 15th of September that same year, one of the prophets in

14

training called and gave me the sad news that she had passed away. While spurning prophecy does not always lead to physical death, it can also lead to unnecessary dry seasons, lack, spiritual death, unhappiness and frustration, and significant setbacks in business, ministry, and even our personal life.

The main reasons for confusion in prophetic revelations include, but are not limited to, the vessel, the receiver, or the mishandling of the gifts due to immaturity, misunderstanding, or presumption.

WHEN THE PROPHECY IS HINDERED

In 2 Kings 3, King Jehoram and King Jehoshaphat sought a word from Elisha, the Prophet, on how they could attack the King of Moab, hoping for victory. According to verse 18, Elisha replied:

"18 And this is a simple matter in the sight of the Lord, he will deliver the Moabites into your hand.

19Also you shall attack every fortified city and choice city and shall cut down every good tree and stop up every spring of water and ruin every good piece of land with stones".

The scripture shows that the battle went oppositely from what the Prophet had prophesied.

26And when the king of Moab saw that the battle was too fierce for him, he took with him seven hundred men who drew sword to break through to the King of Edom, but they could not.

27 Then he took his eldest son who would have reigned in his place and offered him as a burnt offering upon the wall, and there was great indignation against Israel. So, they departed from him and returned to their own land.

The sacrifice interfered with the fulfillment of the prophetic word; hence Israel did not prevail. Resentment overtook the would-be shouts of victory as the King of Moab did the unthinkable; he sacrificed his firstborn heir upon the wall.

Despite this, the scripture did not discredit Elisha as being a prophet. In contrast, it can help us see that a prophet is not necessarily false based on the prophecy. If viewed as a learning tool, it can bring a better understanding to the body of Christ and enlighten us on spiritual matters. *1 Corinthians 13: 9* declares, *"For we know in part, and we prophesy in part."*

WHEN THE RECEIVER 'MISSES'!

According to *2 Kings 20:12-19*, when King Hezekiah got sick, an envoy from Babylon went to see him. He showed them all the treasures– the silver, gold, spice, and precious ointment that Israel had. There was nothing in his palace or in all his kingdom that Hezekiah did not show them. Subsequently, a prophetic word released by the Prophet Isaiah to King Hezekiah highlighted a prophecy that the children of Israel would be in captivity. King Hezekiah replied, *"The word of the Lord which you have spoken is good!"* He added, *"Will there not be peace and truth at least in my days?"*

King Hezekiah, like many of us, received prophetic words from the Lord and misinterpreted them, and intellectualized the words. We miss that our actions have consequences and will impact our lives and the lives of many around us. As a result, we blame the vessels or even God himself for our immaturity. As much as possible, record your prophecies or ask someone what was said and note it, giving special attention to them lest we pray like King Hezekiah.

There are many instances in the Bible where prophecies were overturned, failed, and aborted; discussing those instances would take me another book to break down. However, as prophetic vessels, we must rise to a higher standard of understanding, accurately determining whether the word is of the Lord and whether it is for the sake of our destiny. This book will help you to identify different sources from which prophecies can come. It will show you how to avoid wrong marriages, wrong destinations, wrong choices, wrong company, and even false elevation.

The mishandling of the gifts

The gifts are mishandled due to immaturity, misunderstanding, presumption, idolatry, and the *'prostituting'* of the gospel.

Immaturity

An immature Prophet has not gone through the rigors of the school of the Prophets or reached a certain level of training by God. They are not able to fully execute the prophetic office. The story of Elisha and Elijah is a classic example of a prophet training another prophet. Elijah, the mentor prophet found Elisha working in his father's field *(1 Kings 19:19)*; he summoned the young man by wrapping his cloak around him, summoning him as his apprentice.

1 Kings 19: 19- 21

19 So, he departed thence, and found Elisha the son of Shaphat, who was plowing with twelve yoke of oxen before him, and he with the twelfth: and Elijah passed by him, and cast his mantle upon him.

²⁰ *And he left the oxen, and ran after Elijah, and said, let me, I pray thee, kiss my father and my mother, and then I will follow thee. And he said unto him, go back again: for what have I done to thee?*

²¹ *And he returned back from him, and took a yoke of oxen, and slew them, and boiled their flesh with the instruments of the oxen, and gave unto the people, and they did eat. Then he arose, and went after Elijah, and ministered unto him.*

It is clear from 2 *Kings* 2 that there were schools of the Prophets at Bethel, Jericho, and Jordon.

The Bible shares training experiences endured by the Prophets Ezekiel and Jeremiah. Let us look at Jeremiah's background; see *Jeremiah 1: 11- 15. Moreover, the word of the LORD came unto me, saying, Jeremiah, what seest thou? And I said, I see a rod of an almond tree.*

¹¹ *Then said the LORD unto me, Thou hast well seen: for I will hasten my word to perform it.*

¹² *And the word of the LORD came unto me the second time, saying, What seest thou? And I said, I see a seething pot, and the face thereof is toward the north.*

13 *Then the* LORD *said unto me, Out of the north an evil shall break forth upon all the inhabitants of the land.*

14 *For, lo, I will call all the families of the kingdoms of the north, saith the* LORD; *and they shall come, and they shall set every one his throne at the entering of the gates of Jerusalem, and against all the walls thereof round about, and against all the cities of Judah*

One way the Lord trains Prophets is by taking them to His secret place and employing a question and answer method. This questioning shows their level of understanding and interpretation/revelation of what is seen or heard. It also acts as a confidence booster as, eventually, they will have to declare the word of the Lord with boldness and confidence.

Misunderstanding

When Prophetic revelations are misunderstood, there is not enough maturity to understand what is seen or heard. *Genesis 40* introduces the butler, the baker, and Joseph in prison. Joseph interpreted their bewildering dreams. Seeking guidance from someone more mature than you may resolve misunderstandings in the prophetic ministry.

Presumption

Presumption is best defined as speaking before God reveals what you see or hear. See *Deuteronomy 18: 22 (NKJV)*, which states:

22 *When a prophet speaks in the name of the* LORD, *if the thing does not happen or come to pass, that is the thing which the* LORD *has not spoken; the prophet has spoken it presumptuously; you shall not be afraid of him.*

Idolizing the gift

When you idolize the gift, you depend more on the gift than the gift giver, God. At this stage, the spiritual disciplines of prayer, fasting and reading the word become almost nonexistent as the prophet focuses more on what they hear directly. The downfall is that without fasting, prayer, and reading the word, one can tap off into *divination* without knowing. Prayer and fasting act as a gauge that governs the gift. Jesus mentions this in the bible in *St. Matthew 7: 22* when he said, *"Many will say to me in that day, Lord, Lord, have we not prophesied in thy name? and in thy name have cast out devils? And in thy name done many wonderful works?*

21

Jesus was talking mainly about those who have no relationship with him but focus on the gift.

Prostituting the Gift

When one *'prostitutes'* the gift, their motives become impure. They no longer prophesy to edify the body; instead, they prophesy for financial needs. Micah 3: 11 says:

[11] *The heads thereof judge for reward, and the priests thereof teach for hire, and the prophets thereof divine for money: yet will they lean upon the LORD, and say, is not the LORD among us? None evil can come upon us.*

Let us take heed so that we do not mishandle the gifts.

Chapter 2

Did God say that?

Coming from a very prophetic family and as a prophet myself, I have learned to discern the sources of prophecies through trial and error. There needs to be a willingness to allow the Holy Spirit to teach us, and we must be receptive enough to allow the eyes of our understanding to be enlightened with biblical knowledge of spiritual things. This understanding and enlightenment will ensure that we become fully equipped on what prophecies to accept and what to ignore.

Many Christians have ignored the seriousness of discerning the source of a prophetic word, and if we are willing to confess, then it is accurate to say that such Christians are living a life full of misery. False hope and disappointments have quickly followed those who fail to discern the source of a prophetic word. As a result, many have blamed God and have turned away from the faith. False prophecies can cause a delay in one's life and can result in a shifting of purpose.

At the beginning of my ministry, I attended a prayer conference. However, a week before, while I was in prayer, I heard the Lord say, "I have called you to be the head and not the tail," as stated in *Deuteronomy 28:13*. As I continued to pray, He said, "don't allow anyone to tell you otherwise." Being young and immature, I did not understand what the Lord was saying, but I kept it close to my heart. I sat around the table amongst five young ministers on the conference day.

A lady came and grabbed me and another minister and said to the other minister, "The Lord has called you to travel the world like Abraham."

She then told me that I would be his armor-bearer and that I should not leave his side but travel with him wherever he went. Then the Lord brought back to my remembrance what He said to me in secret, and at that moment, in my mind, I started to question the word given to me.

On another occasion, I faced a major decision in the immature stage of my ministry. I knew I heard the Lord but was not confident enough to stand on what I heard; then, the prophecies started coming. About ten prophets said it was God, and another ten said to be careful because it was not.

24

Young, confused, concerned, stuck, and at my lowest point, a lady came by my house and said the Lord sent her. She began speaking in tongues and started prophesying to the point where I started crying because I felt what I thought was the Spirit of God. Her word of knowledge was accurate, and she told me my decision was wrong and that I should wait. I believed every word she said and neglected to act on what I heard in my spirit, which caused me two years of delay.

The Lord told me later that if something sounds real, it does not mean it is the truth. It took me another two years for the same opportunity to present itself.

Chapter 3

Seven Sources of Prophecy

This chapter highlights seven sources of Prophecy.
They are as follows:

Concern

The word concern is associated with fear, impulsiveness, and emotional anxiety. As we walk this Christian journey with our Lord Jesus Christ, we will encounter persons who love us and become close to us; they will get to know us to a certain extent. As friendship bonds form and close relationships knit, we start to care for each other and sometimes get concerned with one another's issues.

In these instances, emotions can begin to override discernment. The closeness and familiarity sometimes act as a barrier, preventing correct discernment and the issuing of an accurate word to that friend. Family can release a word out of fear of a loved one making the wrong decision based on personal experience. Instances of this are common when it comes on to marriage.

Samson's Philistine Wife

Judges 14:1-3

¹Now, Samson went down to Timnah and saw a woman in Timnah of the daughters of the Philistines.

² So, he went up and told his father and mother, saying, "I have seen a woman in Timnah of the daughters of the Philistines; now therefore, get her for me as a wife."

³ Then his father and mother said to him, "Is there no woman among the daughters of your brethren, or among all my people, that you must go and get a wife from the uncircumcised Philistines? And Samson said to his father, "Get her for me, for [a]she pleases me well."

⁴ But his father and mother did not know that it was of the LORD—that He was seeking an occasion to move against the Philistines. For at that time, the Philistines had dominion over Israel.

Samson was getting ready to make a decision that God wanted him to make for his glory, but his parents were against it because of cultural differences or the fear of damage coming to their home. Family members can be against God's ordained decisions because of differences in age, background, financial status, et *cetera*.

Prophecy vs Discernment

We must consider scripture and align our ideals accordingly, as much as we love our family members. *Samuel 17: 7* declares, *"the LORD does not see as man sees; for man looks at the outward appearance, but the LORD looks at the heart."*

Divination

The spirit of divination is a source that many have prophesied from unknowingly. The word from this source may seem real and mind-blowing, but it isn't true. People who usually operate with a familiar spirit provide a level of accuracy to grab the hearer's attention to open them up to deception.

A minister of the gospel can unknowingly operate under the spirit of divination if he or she loses the discipline to study the Bible or pray as the Lord leads. This type of spirit is deceptive and self-seeking, and it will bring false hope, which eventually leads to open shame if someone is led astray by divination.

Act 16: 16 -19 (NKJV)

[16]Now it happened, as we went into prayer, that a certain slave girl possessed with a spirit of divination met us, who brought her masters much profit by fortune-telling.

[17] This girl followed Paul and us, and cried out, saying, "These men are the servants of the Most High God, who proclaim to us the way of salvation."

[18] And this she did for many days. But Paul, greatly [d]annoyed, turned and said to the spirit, "I command you in the name of Jesus Christ to come out of her." And he came out that very hour.

[19] But when her masters saw that their hope of profit was gone, they seized Paul and Silas and dragged them into the marketplace to the authorities.

If the Apostle Paul didn't have the spirit of discernment, people would have thought that she was a prophetess sent by the Lord to confirm their mission. The information she released was accurate but masked by the enemy's tactics. It was a simple tactic to bring distraction to their assignment.

Flesh

Prophecies that come from the flesh can excite the hearer. However, it is aligned with ungodly desires and doesn't bear witness to the Spirit of God. These types of prophecies are momentary and very misleading.

For example, *1 Samuel 16:5-7* states

29

5 *And he said, "Peaceably; I have come to sacrifice to the LORD. Sanctify yourselves and come with me to the sacrifice." Then he consecrated Jesse and his sons and invited them to the sacrifice.*

6 *So it was, when they came, that he looked at Eliab and said, "Surely the LORD's anointed is before Him!"* 7 *But the LORD said to Samuel, "Do not look at his appearance or at his physical stature, because I have refused him. For the LORD does not see as man sees; for man looks at the outward appearance, but the LORD looks at the heart."*

Samuel was one of the most accurate prophets of God. God told him that *not one* of his words would fall to the ground. He was sent to the house of Jesse, the father of David, to anoint the next king over Israel. As soon as Samuel saw Eliab, David's older brother, he automatically made a traditional, fleshy assumption. He thought this was the choice of the Lord because he looked fit for the throne based on his appearance; he was good-looking and physically fit because he was in the military.

God then made a profound statement to Samuel; He told him not to look at this fleshly appearance since God knows the heart of men. God wanted to make a change since his people were suffering at the hand of Saul's leadership. Saul was good-looking like Eliab but wasn't strong enough in the heart to put his will aside and conform to God's will and fulfill God's purpose.

Deception

The spirit of deception is a broad topic in the prophetic. It is a complete book by itself. The word *deception* means to use cunning means to gain a particular result. *Spiritual deception* means manipulating a situation to turn it from God's original plan.

Deception comes from the devil and originates from our flesh through dreams, visions, random thoughts, lying lips, *et cetera*. As I stated before, a believer must have the gift of discernment. It is a lifesaver as we draw closer to the end times.

In one season of my life, stuck in the valley of decisions, my heart was towards business. However, the word of the Lord was *"ministry and not business."* I battled with the Lord internally since I was a better businessman than a Minister of the Gospel. It was easier to trust in my ability than in God since I wasn't confident in public speaking and did not know how to express myself.

I said yes to ministry with my lips, but I didn't trust God enough in my heart. While struggling, I went to bed, and a man appeared to me and said to me, "business and not ministry." Convinced that the approval was for business, I set my mind toward that. Until later, in prayer about the matter, I heard the audible voice of the Lord instructing me not to walk away from what He had called me to do. I was puzzled until the Lord revealed that the enemy entered my dream, fueled by the attraction of my desire for business in a bid to deceive me.

There is a well-known Bible story about a young and old prophet (1 Kings 13:11-25). Many would assume that the old Prophet was the more senior Prophet, and the young Prophet was the more youthful Prophet, but the Bible did not say senior (older) or younger, which shows that the story wasn't about age. It is safe to say that the old Prophet referred to a prophet God formally used before he started using the young Prophet.

It could be that the older Prophet held on to traditions, so God had to call someone more receptive to the new things He was doing and willing to speak what he said. Jealousy ensued in the old Prophet, and as a result, he deceived the younger Prophet by telling him that an Angel of the Lord appeared to him and asked him to extend an invitation to the young Prophet, whom God strictly warned not to eat or drink in the city. The young

Prophet fell for the deception, which cut his ministry and cost him his life.

Deception can come from anyone with a hidden motive. It usually precedes a significant accomplishment or follows an outstanding achievement as it aims to divert one's attention from the plan of the Lord. Let us look at Nehemiah.

Nehemiah, one of the greatest discerners in the Bible, was sent by God to rebuild the walls and gates of Jerusalem. While completing this God-given assignment, enemies rose against him. They went as far as to mock him saying that the wall is not strong enough to hold a fox to discourage him from completing his assignment. After the deception through discouragement failed, Noadiah, a prophetess, was hired to deceive through her prophecies.

Nehemiah 6:11-14

[11] *And I said, "Should such a man as I flee? And who is there, such as I, who would go into the temple to save his life? I will not go in!"*

[12] *Then I perceived that God had not sent him at all but that he pronounced this prophecy against me because Tobiah and Sanballat had hired him.*

13For this reason, he was hired, that I should be afraid and act that way and sin, so that they might have cause for an evil report, that they might reproach me.

14 My God, remember Tobiah and Sanballat, according to these their works, and the prophetess Noadiah and the rest of the prophets who would have made me afraid.

Interestingly, the Bible exposes the fact that the prophetess Noadiah was for hire and facilitated the deception by lying in the name of the Lord. The deception was intended to thwart Nehemiah's efforts and usher him to stop what God had told him to start, but God is not the author of confusion.

The Heart

Prophecy from the heart is very common amongst believers, and many cannot discern when a prophetic word is from this source. Societal upbringing and life teach us that it's okay to follow our heart or to follow what the heart says.

The Bible teaches us differently; let's look at what the Bible says about the heart. *He who trusts in his own heart is a fool, but whoever walks wisely will be delivered. (Proverbs 28:26)*

What we have been taught by society gives us a level of comfort or self-assurance, but that is now being challenged by the Bible. Another scripture in *Jeremiah 17:9-1* declares, *" The heart is deceitful above all things, and desperately wicked; Who can know it?"*

Any prophecy from the heart can be far from the truth; in the book of Jeremiah, the prophets were prophesying comfort to a rebellious people, which would have encouraged them in their madness, but the Spirit of God was saying something different. One reason the prophets prophesied comfort is that no prophet felt comfortable prophesying destruction to God's people, so compromising was easier.

Nevertheless, as prophetic vessels, we must say what God is saying without compromising because people's lives are at stake.

Atmosphere

Prophesies from the atmosphere are very common in the church culture. Many have had the experience of this type of prophecy without being aware of it. A prophetic vessel that is not mature in the prophetic, invited as a guest speaker to a church or a conference, has to discern or detect the mixed emotions of the leader or the congregation and will often make the mistake of saying the "Lord says."

A guest speaker can also discern what is in the leader's heart and prophesy, but it does not mean that it is coming from the realm of heaven. Let us look at two examples from the Bible.

1 Kings 22:1-40

1 Now, three years passed without war between Syria and Israel. 2 Then it came to pass, in the third year, that Jehoshaphat, the king of Judah, went down to visit the king of Israel.

3 And the king of Israel said to his servants, "Do you know that Ramoth in Gilead is ours, but we hesitate to take it out of the hand of the king of Syria?"

4 So, he said to Jehoshaphat, "Will you go with me to fight at Ramoth Gilead?" Jehoshaphat said to the king of Israel, "I am as you are, my people as your people, my horses as your horses."

5 Also, Jehoshaphat said to the king of Israel, "Please inquire for the word of the LORD today."

⁶ *Then the king of Israel gathered the prophets together, about four hundred men, and said to them, "Shall I go against Ramoth Gilead to fight, or shall I refrain?" So, they said, "Go up, for the Lord will deliver it into the hand of the king."*

⁷ *And Jehoshaphat said, "Is there not still a prophet of the LORD here, that we may inquire of Him?"*

⁸ *So, the king of Israel said to Jehoshaphat, "There is still one man, Micaiah the son of Imlah, by whom we may inquire of the LORD; but I hate him, because he does not prophesy good concerning me, but evil."*
And Jehoshaphat said, "Let not the king say such things!"

⁹ *Then the king of Israel called an officer and said, "Bring Micaiah the son of Imlah quickly!"*

¹⁰ *The king of Israel and Jehoshaphat, the king of Judah, having put on their robes, sat each on his throne, at a threshing floor at the entrance of the gate of Samaria; and all the prophets prophesied before them.*

¹¹ *Now Zedekiah, the son of Chenaanah, had made horns of iron for himself; and he said, "Thus says the LORD: 'With these you shall gore the Syrians until they are destroyed.'"*

37

12 *And all the prophets prophesied so, saying, "Go up to Ramoth Gilead and prosper, for the LORD will deliver it into the king's hand."*

13 *Then the messenger who had gone to call Micaiah spoke to him, saying, "Now listen, the words of the prophets with one accord encourage the king. Please, let your word be like the word of one of them, and speak encouragement."*

14 *And Micaiah said, "As the LORD lives, whatever the LORD says to me, that I will speak."*

15 *Then he came to the king; and the king said to him, "Micaiah, shall we go to war against Ramoth Gilead, or shall we refrain?" And he answered him, "Go and prosper, for the LORD will deliver it into the hand of the king!"*

16 *So, the king said to him, "How many times shall I make you swear that you tell me nothing but the truth in the name of the LORD?"*

17 *Then he said, "I saw all Israel scattered on the mountains, as sheep that have no shepherd. And the LORD said, 'These have no master. Let each return to his house in peace."*

¹⁸ *And the king of Israel said to Jehoshaphat, "Did I not tell you he would not prophesy good concerning me, but evil?"*

¹⁹ *Then Micaiah said, "Therefore hear the word of the LORD: I saw the LORD sitting on His throne, and all the host of heaven standing by, on His right hand and on His left.*

²⁰ *And the LORD said, 'Who will persuade Ahab to go up, that he may fall at Ramoth Gilead?' So, one spoke in this manner, and another spoke in that manner.*

²¹ *Then a spirit came forward and stood before the LORD, and said, 'I will persuade him.'*

²² *The LORD said to him, 'In what way?' So, he said, 'I will go out and be a lying spirit in the mouth of all his prophets.' And the LORD said, you shall persuade him, and also prevail. Go out and do so.'*

²³ *Therefore look! The LORD has put a lying spirit in the mouth of all these prophets of yours, and the LORD has declared disaster against you."*

²⁴ *Now Zedekiah, the son of Chenaanah, went near and struck Micaiah on the cheek and said, "Which way did the spirit from the LORD go from me to speak to you?"*

²⁵ And Micaiah said, "Indeed, you shall see on that day when you go into an inner chamber to hide!"

²⁶ So, the king of Israel said, "Take Micaiah, and return him to Amon, the governor of the city, and to Joash, the king's son;

²⁷ And say, 'Thus says the king: "Put this fellow in prison, and feed him with bread of affliction and water of affliction until I come in peace."

²⁸ But Micaiah said, "If you ever return in peace, the LORD has not spoken by me." And he said, "Take heed, all you people!"

Ahab Dies in Battle *(also found in (2 Chr. 18:28–34)*

²⁹ So, the king of Israel and Jehoshaphat, the king of Judah, went up to Ramoth Gilead.

³⁰ And the king of Israel said to Jehoshaphat, "I will disguise myself and go into battle; but you put on your robes." So, the king of Israel disguised himself and went into battle.

³¹ Now, the king of Syria had commanded the thirty-two captains of his chariots, saying, "Fight with no one small or great, but only with the king of Israel."

32 So it was, when the captains of the chariots saw Jehoshaphat, that they said, "Surely it is the king of Israel!" Therefore, they turned aside to fight against him, and Jehoshaphat cried out.

33 And it happened, when the captains of the chariots saw that it was not the king of Israel, that they turned back from pursuing him.

34 Now, a certain man drew a bow at random and struck the king of Israel between the joints of his armor. So, he said to the driver of his chariot, "Turn around and take me out of the battle, for I am wounded."

35 The battle increased that day; and the king was propped up in his chariot, facing the Syrians, and died at evening. The blood ran out from the wound onto the floor of the chariot.

36 Then, as the sun was going down, a shout went throughout the army, saying, "Every man to his city, and every man to his own country!"

37 So, the king died and was brought to Samaria. And they buried the king in Samaria.

38 Then someone washed the chariot at a pool in Samaria, and the dogs licked up his blood while the harlots bathed, according to the word of the LORD which He had spoken.

39 Now the rest of the acts of Ahab, and all that he did, the ivory house which he built and all the cities that he built, are they not written in the book of the chronicles of the kings of Israel?

40 So Ahab rested with his fathers. Then Ahaziah, his son reigned in his place.

The king's heart wanted victory, and the prophets detected this victory. The prophets were better known as the 400 lying prophets; Micaiah was the only Prophet able to see the decision made in heaven.

Let us look at another example.

"Is Saul among the prophets?" was a common saying in Israel during his reign. This saying came about because Saul ran into a company of prophets twice and started to operate in the prophetic.

1 Samuel 19:23-24

23 So, he went there to Naioth in Ramah. Then the Spirit of God was upon him also, and he went on and prophesied until he came to Naioth in Ramah.

24 And he also stripped off his clothes and prophesied before Samuel in like manner, and lay down naked all that day and all that night. Therefore, they say, "Is Saul also among the prophets?"

Saul was angry with David and started chasing him. When Saul entered Ramah, the prophets had already created an atmosphere where the Spirit of God was present. Saul, rejected as a king, was still able to prophesy in the atmosphere he entered. We can find comfort in this as believers, that we can lean on an atmosphere where the presence of God is to get revelation from God about a current situation.

Spirit of God

The Spirit of God is the source from which all authentic sources of prophecy come. Whenever someone prophesies to you by the Spirit of God, you can rest assured that you will be set free. Prophecy from the Spirit of God gives direction and revelation to a person's life. For a prophetic vessel to effectively prophesy by the Spirit of God, one must be pure, that is, living a godly lifestyle, praying, fasting, and studying the Bible.

In the Old Testament days, the Spirit of the Lord would come upon a vessel and proclaim the word of the Lord.

In the New Testament, the comforter which dwells within believers speaks from within. In other words, the

Holy Spirit dwells within once you are born again. The Holy Spirit enables all believers to prophesy even though Church leaders did not declare the calling of a prophet over their lives. Whether it is the word of knowledge, wisdom, gift of faith, healing, working of miracles, prophecy, discerning of Spirit, diverse kinds of tongues, and interpretation of tongues, they all come from one Spirit, the Spirit of God.

The Spirit of God brings light into human lives and accesses our dark areas to bring transformation. When a vessel prophesies to you by the Spirit of God, the following will occur: your spirit man is encouraged and cheered; healing for the brokenhearted; liberation in one's life and the untying of those bound for years.

It also facilitates speedy remedies to situations. All the mighty vessels used to do wonders in the Bible were vessels filled with the Spirit of God. For example, Jahaziel was not a prophet but a vessel that God used to encourage Jehoshaphat when the army of the Ammon, Moab, and Mount Seir rose against him.

According to *2 Chronicles 20:14-17*

¹⁴ *Then the Spirit of the LORD came upon Jahaziel the son of Zechariah, the son of Benaiah, the son of Jeiel, the son of*

Mattaniah, a Levite of the sons of Asaph, in the midst of the assembly.

¹⁵ And he said, "Listen, all you of Judah and you inhabitants of Jerusalem, and you, King Jehoshaphat! Thus says the LORD to you: Do not be afraid nor dismayed because of this great multitude, for the battle is not yours, but God's.

¹⁶ Tomorrow go down against them. They will surely come up by the Ascent of Ziz, and you will find them at the end of the brook before the Wilderness of Jeruel.

¹⁷ You will not need to fight in this battle. Position yourselves, stand still and see the salvation of the LORD, who is with you, O Judah and Jerusalem!' Do not fear or be dismayed; tomorrow, go out against them, for the LORD is with you."

Chapter 4

Prophecy as a Gift

Contrary to popular belief, you don't have to be a prophet to prophesy. The gift of prophecy is for every believer who has received the Holy Spirit and is available for God's use.

Prophecy is the foretelling of a future. The gift of prophecy is the only gift the Bible permits us to covet after *(1 Corinthians 14:39).* The prophetic was first biblically introduced to us by God himself. Journey with me to the book of *Genesis 1:3;* "...*then God said, "Let there be light," and there was light."*

Therefore, brethren desire earnestly to prophesy (see 1 Corinthians 14:39). Paul the Apostle encourages all believers to desire the gift of prophecy above all other supernatural gifts. This gift, given by the Holy Spirit to believers, involves proclaiming revelation from God to others to build them up.

According to the Prophet's dictionary by Paula A. Price, prophecy is "an inspired communication from God. It is God's supernatural communicative media. What makes it a prophecy is that God speaks through his prophets before the earthly events in question occur."

Every believer, filled with the Holy Ghost, can prophesy. God gave his only begotten son to us as a gift, and his only begotten Son, who is Jesus Christ, also gave us the gift of the Holy Spirit. The Holy Spirit also gave us gifts, and one of the gifts was the gift of prophecy.

The Holy Spirit can pass down the gift of prophecy in three ways:

As an Inheritance

When I call to remembrance the genuine faith that is in you, which dwelt first in your grandmother Lois and your mother Eunice, and I am persuaded is in you also. (2 Timothy 1:5) Paul, a mentor to Timothy, reminded him that the gift of faith was a gift in the lineage, first in his grandmother, then his mother, and now in him. Often, we focus on generational curses and miss the generational blessing. *A good man leaves an inheritance to his children's children* according to *Proverbs 13:22*. This verse indicates that bloodlines can be conduits to pass down God's gifts, given that there is impartation and activation.

By Impartation

For I long to see you, that I may impart to you some spiritual gift, so that you may be established (Romans 1:11). In this scripture, Paul the Apostle clearly shows us how important it is to have spiritual gifts *imparted* unto us. A spiritual gift not only establishes but also brings expansion. According to *Proverb 18:16, "a man's gift makes room for him, and it brings him in the presence of great men."*

At the lowest point of Timothy's ministry, he was up against opposition due to his age and for being a gentile. Paul then reminded him to fan into flame the gift of God that was in him by the laying of hands. We need to receive impartation as believers; it opens and unlocks us into a different dimension and gives us spiritual access to insights we did not have before.

By Grace

Having then gifts, differing according to the grace that is given to us, let us use them: Roman 12:6 (NKJV)

Whenever God provides an individual with an assignment, He also grants spiritual gifts to help equip the believer for the task. With God's grace to complete the assignment, He also gives us gifts. These gifts are catalytic in making the job easier and ensuring completion.

These are two examples for more clarification.

Example 1

Amos 7:14-15

¹⁴ *Then answered Amos, and said to Amaziah, I was no prophet, neither was I a prophet's son; but I was an herdman, and a gatherer of sycomore fruit:*

¹⁵ *And the LORD took me as I followed the flock, and the LORD said unto me, Go, prophesy unto my people Israel.*

God called Amos into the prophetic at a time when he wanted to show His people justice. Amos testified that he was not a prophet, which shows that he wasn't made aware that God would use him. Unlike Jeremiah, predestined to be a prophet, Amos' calling was different since he was a faithful shepherd available for use when needed. God graced him for the season to complete that assignment.

Example 2

Acts 1:24-26

[24] And they prayed and said, "You, O Lord, who know the hearts of all, show which of these two You have chosen

[25] to take part in this ministry and apostleship from which Judas by transgression fell, that he might go to his own place."

[26] And they cast their lots, and the lot fell on Matthias. And he was numbered with the eleven apostles.

After Judas had betrayed Christ and hanged himself, God's vineyard needed an apostle so the work of the Lord could continue. Mathias, who was just a disciple, was now promoted to the office of the apostleship because his heart was in the right place with God. Often, we forget that God uses whoever is available and not those who think they are capable.

David was not God's first choice, but Saul's willful disobedience caused the Lord to select a new king to shepherd his people. Having the gift of prophecy means you can use your tongue as a pen to write new chapters in your life and the lives of others. The gift of prophecy gives us access to things ahead of time, which gives us time to prepare to receive.

As a believer, I try to live a prophesied life as Jesus did. From birth to death and resurrection, the life of Jesus was prophesied. Once the gift of prophecy is in operation, it eliminates darkness and brings light to one's life for comfort, edification, and exhortation. If you can't prophesy yet, get close to someone who does.

Everyone should be excited to hear what God has in store for their future. May God use you mightily to prophesy for His glory to change the lives of your family member, friends, and even strangers.

Chapter 5

The Gift of Discernment

The gift of discernment is a unique and distinct gift needed in our everyday lives. Most believers mainly focus on the gift of prophecy and the gift of tongues while neglecting the gift of discernment. While prophecy and the gift of tongues are very powerful, without discernment, you cannot tell if a prophecy is true or false and if a tongue is unknown, angelic, or demonic. So, what is discernment?

The Greek word for discernment is *diakrisis* which means to judge or distinguish. As stated in the previous chapter, the gift of prophecy is the only gift God permitted us to covet. The gift of discernment was the only gift God said he was pleased with when requested by Solomon.

After King David's passing away, his son King Solomon inherited the Kingdom and became the shepherd to lead the people of Israel. What seems to be an excellent achievement for Solomon could have also resulted in disgrace or bloodshed, as his father had left him many enemies. He was the youngest of several brothers; by tradition, he shouldn't have become king, and his father's advisors were also wicked.

Solomon, who was about 20 years of age according to Jewish writings, was young and inexperienced, facing many challenges that seemed impossible for him to overcome. Then a miracle happened, and while Solomon went to Gibeon to sacrifice to the Lord, he fell asleep, and the Lord appeared to him in a dream and asked him to make a request.

Solomon then asks for a discerning heart to distinguish between right and wrong, and the Lord was pleased by Solomon's request. See *1 Kings 3:5 -15 (NIV)*. The gift of discernment saved Solomon's Kingdom. Solomon knew how difficult it was to judge between right and wrong, and he would need supernatural help from God to fulfill his assignment.

After God imparted the spirit of discernment to Solomon, a test presented itself. Two harlots came to the King with one child claiming the child was theirs; Solomon then asked for a sword to divide the child in two to test the true mother's heart. The woman to whom the child belonged cried out, but the other woman insisted that the king should divide the baby. Then the King discerned that the child belonged to the first lady who cried out. See *1 Kings 3:16 to 27*.

The book of *Hebrew 4:11 to 12* states

¹² *For the word of God is living and powerful, and sharper than any two-edged sword, piercing even to the division of soul and spirit, and of joints and marrow, and is a discerner of the thoughts and intents of the heart.*

The gift of discernment is like a sword sharpened by God's word and given to us to make a sound judgment or distinguish between right or wrong and good and evil.

Is the gift of discernment the same as the discernment of Spirit?

The gift of discernment and the discernment of Spirit are two different gifts that operate on different magnitudes. Some would argue that they are the same, but I beg to differ. Listed among the nine gifts in 1 Corinthians chapter 12 is the discernment of spirit. This Gift focuses mainly on the spirit, whether the Angelic (Genesis 32:22-31), demonic (Act 16:16-19), or the Spirit of the Lord (Judges 6: 34). Let us look at the difference in one story.

God sent a young prophet from Judah to Bethel to warn the king about the evil altar in the city. After the Lord used the young Prophet mightily, he instructed him not to eat food or drink water in the city and then go the way he entered the city. An old prophet in the city heard of all the work the Lord had done through the young Prophet and met him and told him that an angel said he should return to his house and eat and drink, and the young Prophet fell for the trap.

While he was eating, the word of the Lord came to him through the same old Prophet; he had disobeyed the word of the Lord, and he would die. His death was fulfilled. Lack of discernment can lead to physical death like this young Prophet or spiritual death like Adam and Eve in the garden.

If the young Prophet had discernment, he would have known that the older Prophet was telling a lie. If the old Prophet had discernment of spirits, he would have known that the angel that appeared to him, as he said, was not an angel of the Lord because God is not the author of confusion; see *1 Corinthians 14:33*.

As a child of God, the gift of discernment and the discernment of spirit are essential to maneuver your way in the physical and spiritual realms. I once had a coworker who was so wonderful to the human eye, but I always felt something wasn't right with him. I just couldn't discern it fully.

He preached Jesus well, but my gut feelings wouldn't give me peace. Suddenly, the Spirit of the Lord opened my eyes, and I saw a dark angel behind him. I did not understand what it meant until the Lord spoke to me and told me that he was a part of a secret society to which he confessed a few months later.

The gift of discernment placed me on guard while the gift of discernment of spirit revealed that he was working with a spirit that was not of God, and finally, the voice of the Lord brought clarity.

Assumption

Assumption is one of the biggest mistakes prophetic vessels, including discerners, can make. Whenever God reveals something to us, and we do not have the proper interpretation, we should do two things, seek wise counseling, or seek him for the interpretation.

We should always consider that we have a responsibility as prophetic vessels. There are two types of prophets, Nabi and Seer. Nabis are prophets who hear the voice of

God and are often very fluent in speech as they minister the word of the Lord. However, they do not necessarily see in the spiritual realm, while Seers often see in the realm of the spirit.

Seers are more fluent in dreams, open visions, and trances. Seers and Nabis are responsible in the Kingdom because the Lord often speaks in parable to Nabis, and most of the visions Seers see sometimes need interpretation. In the book of *Acts 10:13-15*, Peter had a vision of an unclean animal coming from heaven. Then the Lord spoke to him and said, *"Rise Peter; kill and eat"* Peter misinterpreted the parables as he thought the Lord was forcing him to defile himself.

However, the Lord revealed that he wanted him to bring salvation to the Gentiles. Peter misinterpreted what he saw because he was hungry. He also misinterpreted what he heard. The Lord was saying that He created animals and people alike and that neither should be considered unclean. This vision is often a debating tool among certain denominations.

Let us look at another example of someone who misinterpreted what was said by a prophet in the Bible.

In Isaiah 39:1-8, King Hezekiah was sick, and the King of Babylon sent him his best wishes and a gift. King Hezekiah showed the Babylonian visitors all the treasures in the house of the Lord, and later, Isaiah came to visit and asked him about the visitors. When King Hezekiah told him about all that happened, Isaiah prophesied that Babylon would take all the treasures in his house. However, King Hezekiah thought the prophecy meant peace in his time.

Isaiah the Prophet told the king that Israel would be in captivity in Babylon. I firmly believe that if the king understood the prophecy, prayer and fasting could have overturned that doom. The overturning is similar to what Esther did in her time when there was a plot to wipe out the Jews.

How to use Discernment

The gift of discernment is often used as a weapon in the body of Christ against other believers. You will often hear small talk about a person whose spirit is off or who is struggling with what issues. This gesture will come from someone who seems deep spiritually but is immature. Discernment was never meant to be used to tarnish the character of others or to wave something over someone's head. I knew a lady whose favorite saying was

"I'm picking up something," a cultural slang used to state that she was discerning. However, after a while, her judgment made people feel condemned. We later found that she was operating under a heavy religious spirit.

The Apostle Paul had this issue with the church in Corinth and Rome. He addressed the Church in Rome by saying, *"Who are you to judge another's servant? To his own master, he stands or falls; indeed, he will be made to stand firm, God is able to make him stand" Romans 14:4.*

The Apostle Paul told the church not to use their discernment as a weapon but rather intercede for others because the Lord can keep anyone from falling. The gift is a tool for believers to escape the traps of the enemy. All spiritual gifts are given to us as tools to bring the saints to perfection and guard the work and the assignment of the Kingdom from the enemy's wiles.

Nehemiah is a perfect example of how we should use discernment to protect us from the enemy's schemes which the Bible warns us not to be ignorant of. God sent Nehemiah to the wall of Jerusalem. While he was building the wall, Sanballat, Tobiah, the Arabs, the Ammonites, and the Ashdodites became angry, and they conspired against him with confusion, attacks, distractions, and false prophecies.

Prophecy vs Discernment

Shemaiah was sent to prophesy to Nehemiah to bring fear to him, but Nehemiah discerned that he was a hired prophet assigned to usurp God-given assignments. See *Nehemiah 6:12.*

Chapter 6

When the Gifts Clashes

N ow that we have covered the gift of discernment and the gift of prophecy, let's look at what happens when the gifts clash. Many have asked– can the gifts clash? The answer is in this chapter. As a prophet who has access to many prophets and has trained and equipped prophets and prophetic vessels, I have been asked whether these gifts can clash.

In 2020, I decided to take a trip to Jamaica. As I was getting ready to travel, I had prophets who told me, *"The Lord said don't go to Jamaica,"* while others said, *"after you come back from Jamaica,"* et cetera. At that moment, I became confused and started questioning what the prophets were saying. I knew these prophets were mature, trained, and well-experienced, so I knew they, too, were hearing from God.

Some prophets told me they had seen a car accident that could result in death and a witchcraft attack that could damage my life. I had to ask myself, was I hearing incorrectly from God? I had to seek God more deeply than before. I needed to know what I should do. Why were the prophets saying different things?

I should not go to Jamaica but, on the other hand, when I *"come back from Jamaica."* One morning I woke up and went on my knees; I started praying vigorously because it seemed I had to make a life-or-death decision. My surroundings become unidentifiable whenever I'm in prayer, and the Lord will speak through a vision or audibly to me.

During my prayer time, I went into a trance and saw a man walking up to me in his sandals. His feet were beautiful; fear gripped me, and I wanted to stop what I was seeing, but I could not. Then I heard a voice say, *"it is I; it is I,"* and immediately, I recognized that it was my Lord and Savior, Jesus Christ.

He then spoke to me and said, *"go where I send you, many traps are laid up for you, but you should not be touched; you will go and return untouched."* Then I felt a sense of peace over me, but even so, I still had questions. Nevertheless, I booked my ticket. While I was on the plane, I told myself that the prophets saw the traps the Lord spoke about, yet the Lord still told me to go. Hmmm. I had questions, and I needed answers.

When I arrived in Jamaica, the car that came to pick me up started having electrical and transmission issues. I started saying this is what the prophets saw. Additionally, the territory I was meant to stay in had occultist spirits; one of the demons told me that I didn't belong to this territory, while another appeared to me at the doorway and said I needed to leave.

I told myself these were the reasons the prophets said not to go. I now understood I was up for a fight, but I kept hearing the Lord saying be not afraid; I am with you. After I returned to America, I said there had to be something deeper to this.

While I was in prayer one Sunday morning, the Lord gave me a scenario from the scriptures, which I will discuss soon. After reading the scriptures, the Lord spoke to me, saying, *"Prophecy versus Discernment."* I asked myself if the gifts could clash. I knew the Lord allowed the situation to give an understanding to many who questioned God. It will also help some who have labeled other people that are gifted false because of a lack of understanding. The Church at Corinth had issues with the gift of prophecy and the gift of tongues; while others were prophesying, some would interrupt by speaking in tongues and vice versa. The gifts were now clashing to the point where some started despising both gifts.

The Apostle had to distinguish between the gifts and how to place them in order. The Apostle Paul said the one who prophesies is greater than the one who speaks in tongues unless someone can interpret the tongues. See *1 Corinthians 14:5*. Paul was saying that the gift of prophecy is greater than the gift of tongues, but to solve the rivalry between the two gifts, he then introduced another gift: the interpretation of Tongues.

Paul said the gift of tongues is equal to prophecy when the tongues uttered are interpreted. The gift of prophecy and the gift of discernment are no different. These gifts also clash, but differently, the gift of prophecy can go behind the gift of discernment, and because of this, the discerner will sense danger, then form a conclusion in the name of the Lord.

Psalm 23 verse 4 says Yea, tho I walk through the valley of the shadow of death, I will fear no evil because Thou art with me, your rod and your staff will comfort me. A discerner often discerns death in the valley and says do not take that road; there is damage ahead. Prophecy can say that while you walk through the valley of the shadow of death, you shall fear no evil because God will be with you, and his rod and staff will comfort you.

A discerner can discern danger, but while there is a limit to discernment, the prophecy goes beyond limitations. God will send you through a dangerous path to pull you closer to him or remove fear, doubt, and even unbelief. Paul the Apostle ran into this situation when he was going to Jerusalem, the gifts of discernment and prophecy at work. In Acts 21, Agabus took Paul's belt, bound his hands and feet, and said he would be bound in Jerusalem and delivered up to the Gentiles. After the Prophet and many others discerned the danger, the enemy laid up for Paul in Jerusalem, they begged him not to go the Jerusalem, but Paul did not heed. Then they said, let the will of the Lord be done.

Paul remembered the prophecies released over him that he would be sent to the Gentiles and preach to kings. I would assume that if he had to go to kings, death was not an option for him in Jerusalem because that wasn't his final stop. While reading this as a young minister, I often wondered why Paul disobeyed the prophets' warnings. However, when I started maturing in the Lord, I realized that the experience was not to constrict him but to prepare him for what he would have encountered in Jerusalem.

There was a time in my ministry when I faced persecution from a church I used to attend. It was hard for me as a young man since pain and hurt were screaming from inside of me. People with the gift of discernment could discern what I was going through and started telling me that the church was fighting against me. I felt it was the church's fault based on what the discerner was telling me, but I remembered the word of the Lord that came from a prophetess.
These were her exact words:

"The Lord said you need to submit. Goats fight against authority, but sheep know how to submit" The discerners could pick up what I was going through, but the prophetess was able to see by my pain to instruct me as to what to do. My perspective changed on the situation, and I repented to my leaders and humbled myself.

Chapter 7

Intercession

This chapter will explain how to unite the gifts to get 'sound' results.

As discussed in a previous chapter, the Apostle Paul introduced the gift of interpretation of tongues to end the war between the gift of prophecy and the gift of tongues. Intercession is the way to end the clashing between discernment and prophecy.

Many Christians have been taught that intercession is a gift and only certain people are called to intercede; not only is that statement not true, but it is not biblical. We were all given the mandate to pray and intercede for people, places, regions, nations, and countless other things based on *1 Timothy 2:1-2*. Others are graced more in the area of intercession based on their assignments or the time spent with God.

Interceding is every believer's responsibility. Before I progress further, let us look at what intercession is. The word intercession means to intervene in a matter on someone's behalf. An intercessor is one who stands in the gap for someone or something through prayer or worship to help bring glory to the name of the Lord.

In the book of Genesis, we see a gap between man and God after the fall of humanity. This gap was a result of sin. When Adam was in the garden, there was no need for intercession or prayer because of his intimacy with God. After sin entered, man lost that relationship status with God, but something interesting happened. *Genesis 4:26* says: And *to Seth, to him also there was born a son; and he called his name Enos: then began men to call upon the name of the LORD.*

Man realized there was a need to get back to God, so they started calling on the name of the Lord. This incident marked the first-time intercession was introduced in the Bible.

There was a burden in their hearts to find their way back to God, so they started crying to fill the gap created through sin. God raised prophets and priests to intercede on their behalf. Intercessors often carry burdens for people, nations, and God. They can negotiate with God on behalf of others. It is often said that they can change the mind of God.

Abraham was one of the first persons in the Bible to negotiate with God. *Genesis 18* posits that Abraham was sitting under the tent when three angels appeared to him and declared the word of the Lord to him and made him a promise. The angels were on their way to destroy Sodom and Gomorrah when suddenly, the Lord said, *"should I hide anything from my friend Abraham?"*

The Lord allowed the angels to reveal to Abraham that they were on their way to destroy the city. Abraham remembered that he had his nephew living in the city, so he started interceding.

Abraham began to bargain with the Lord on behalf of the people in the city. He asked the Lord if he could spare the city if he found fifty righteous people; the angels informed him that fifty righteous people were not in the city. Then Abraham went from 45 to 40 to 30 to 20 to 10, then to 5. Abraham's intercession could not save the entire city because of their sinful actions, but God saved some of his family members.

We can learn from Abraham how to be an intercessor. Like Abraham, intercessors are passionate about seeing people saved instead of being destroyed; Abraham challenged God's integrity by asking, *"should a righteous God destroy the righteous with the wicked?"* (Genesis 18:23).

Intercessors often stand between God and judgment, those deserved by a people, the wicked, or against the diabolical scheme for righteousness' sake.

Bold intercessor

In my years of intercession, I have noticed that God, in His extraordinary wisdom, placed many ingredients into making those willing to stand on the forefront to intercede for the Kingdom's sake. Some of those ingredients include compassion, patience, fearlessness, and boldness.

The Children of Israel were stuck in Egypt as enslaved people for four hundred years. After crying out to the Lord for a long time for help, God raised Moses as their deliverer and sent him to them. However, Moses had a few back-and-forth moments with God before accepting the assignment.

We should not view Moses' back and forth with God negatively. Abraham had a similar experience, but Moses' situation was more personal; he understood the bondage from the standpoint of the oppressor and the oppressed.

His confidence was low. He also knew how the system worked in Egypt since he grew up in Pharaoh's house.

Accordingly, he was fearful as he was not a man eloquent in speech. With all of Moses' issues, God saw that he was a man with a heart of compassion. Forty years before, he tried to deliver his brethren from the hands of an Egyptian by killing him.

God then began to build Moses' confidence and removed his fear. Moses achieved this confidence-building and boldness when God sent him to Pharaoh about eight times until he could deliver the children of Israel out of bondage. After reading this story over and over, I asked myself, why didn't God miraculously destroy all the Egyptians and not allow the children of Israel to go through all that back and forth coupled with tribulations without Moses?

I realized later that Moses wasn't only a prophet or a great leader but also an intercessor. As a result of their stubbornness of heart, God had to raise an intercessor, not just any intercessor but also a bold intercessor, to lead them. Let us look at this conversation between God and Moses according to *Exodus 32:7-14*:

"And the Lord said to Moses, "Go, get down! For your people whom you brought out of the land of Egypt have corrupted themselves. They have turned aside quickly out of the way which I commanded them.

They have made themselves a molded calf, and worshiped it and sacrificed to it, and said, 'This is your God, O Israel, that brought you out of the land of Egypt!'" And the Lord said to Moses, "I have seen this people, and indeed it is a stiff-necked people! Now, therefore, let Me alone, that My wrath may burn hot against them, and I may consume them. And I will make of you a great nation." Then Moses pleaded with the Lord his God and said: "Lord, why does your wrath burn hot against Your people whom You have brought out of the land of Egypt with great power and with a mighty hand? Why should the Egyptians speak and say, 'He brought them out to harm them, to kill them in the mountains, and to consume them from the face of the earth'? Turn from your fierce wrath and relent from this harm to your people. Remember Abraham, Isaac, and Israel, your servants, to whom You swore by Your own self, and said to them, 'I will multiply your descendants as the stars of heaven; and all this land that I have spoken of I give to your descendants, and they shall inherit it forever.'" So, the Lord relented from the harm which He said He would do to His people." Some would say that Moses changed God's mind, but let us examine what happened. The same strategies Moses used when God asked him to go to Pharaoh are the strategies he used in asking the Lord not to destroy the children of Israel.

The difference is that he lost the first debate with God, but in this debate, he caused God to turn from his wrath. Moses was bold enough to tell God not to destroy his people and presented strong reasons to support his stance. *Isaiah 41:21* says, *"present your case," says the Lord, "Bring forward your strong reason," say the King of Jacob.* Another version says, *"present your evidence."*

Intercession is like being in a court; God was the judge in this situation, and Moses was the children of Israel's lawyer. The charge was idolatry, which was against the *law*, the first commandment out of the ten commandments. God said to Moses, *"Your people whom you have brought out of Egypt,"* God said I would destroy them. Then Moses challenged God's decision with these statements; he said God, if you destroy them, the nation will hear of it and say that you were unable to do what you promised.

Moses closed the case by saying, *"Remember your covenant you made with Abraham, Isaac, and Jacob."* Moses knew that God was a covenant-keeping God according to his word. (*Deuteronomy 5:10*).

Chapter 8

Tools for Intercession

The following are tools that God has given us to address the matter of intercession.

• **Bible**- The word of God is one of the most potent tools in intercession; Christians must know the Bible to be effective in every area of their lives.

In *Hebrew 4:12*, the word of God is described as *"quick and powerful and sharper than any two-edged sword, piercing even to the dividing asunder of soul and Spirit and of the joints and marrow, and is a discerner of thoughts and intents of the heart."*

In *Ephesians 6:12 to 18*, we are instructed to wear the Armor of God so we can win the war against the enemy. The sword of the spirit, which is the word of God (the Bible), is a vital part of the armor. It is a powerful weapon that can be used to attack the enemy, and most importantly, it is our guideline as Christians; as such, our prayers must be directed by the word of God.

• **Knowledge**- *Hosea 4:6* says, *"my people are destroyed for lack of knowledge."*

We need the knowledge of the word of God to intercede or fight warfare effectively. This knowledge will be magnified when coupled with the physical and spiritual insight of the assignment. For example, Daniel was a great intercessor who prayed thrice daily. When he realized that the exile was supposed to end after 70 years, according to *Daniel 9:1-2* and *Jeremiah 29:10*, he turned his face to the temple of God in Jerusalem. According to the prayer of Solomon in *2 Chronicles 6:20*, when Israel turns their face to the temple, God should hear them regardless of their sins.

God then sealed Solomon's prayer with a promise in *2 Chronicles 7:14*, where he stated:

> *If my people, which are called by my name, shall humble themselves, and pray, and seek my face, and turn from their wicked ways; then will I hear from heaven, and will forgive their sin, and will heal their land.*

Daniel had to study the scroll to find out about the prophecy Jeremiah declared about the exile and searched the scrolls to know the promise God made to Solomon. Similarly, for present-day purposes, an intercessor must be willing to study patterns, cycles, and systems to have a strategy to pray.

• **Fasting** – Throughout biblical history, during a war between kings or nations against nations, and even in the New Testament, during spiritual warfare, the Lord instructed his people to call a fast. Fasting is a mystery; one would ask why we should be fasting during intercession since we need our strength to pray or to wage war. The answer is simple when Zerubbabel faced an insurmountable challenge, the word of the Lord came to him, saying, not by might nor by power but by my Spirit (*Zechariah 4:6*). Whenever you fast, it is a signal of humility and a signal to God that your strength is not good enough, and His help is needed. Fasting heightens spiritual senses, making us keener to the things of the Spirit and changing the battle from the realm of the flesh to the realm of the Spirit.

Fasting can:
- overturn evil verdict (book of Esther)
- scatter those who gather against you (2 Chronicles 20)
- turn the wrath of God from nations (Book of Jonah)

- bring forth divine connection (Act 14:23)
- overcome temptation (Matthew 4)
- unlock mystery (Daniel 10)
- shut the mouth of the accusers (Daniel 6)
- secure safety (Act 27:33)

Conclusion

This book is merely a prelude to further revelations God wants to share with you, His child. As I highlight the marked difference between prophecy and discernment, note that this holds open the door of edification for the body of Christ. There is no doubt that it is an area that demands clarity.

To better understand prophetic utterances and eliminate confusion in prophetic revelations, we need to examine the varying stakeholders- the vessel and the receiver and how we handle the gifts in general. Correctly hearing and interpreting the voice of God is paramount in prophetic circles and would bid us ask, did God say that?

One of these seven sources of prophecies highlighted, including concern, divination, flesh, deception, the heart, the atmosphere, and the spirit of God, may be the channel through which the word of God comes. Either way, prophecy should be seen as a gift that every believer should crave after. The Bible conveys that the gift of prophecy may be transferred to the believer via inheritance, impartation, or grace.

There is yet another gift that acts as the litmus test for Prophecy, whether it is true or false. The gift of discernment places the believer on guard to be able to distinguish what is really of God. Too often, we confuse the discernment of gift with the discernment of spirit. The latter focuses on whether the spirit detected is angelic, demonic, or Lord's Spirit. All this sensitivity to the Lord's voice will allow us to distinguish between spirits.

One of the biggest mistakes discerners can make is to assume. Avoid this trap and seek wise counseling or God for the interpretation. We must handle the whole matter of discernment well; the gift is for the edification of the body of Christ and should at no point become a beating stick for our fellow laborers in Christ.

There are times when the gift of discernment and the gift of prophecy would appear to clash but always bear in mind that intercession is the key that will unite the gifts to provide the desired results from God. May the ingredients of a good intercessor: compassion, patience, fearlessness, and boldness, be your lot as you employ the tools of intercession to get the best results for you and your church family.

Stay in Touch

Facebook: Richard Rowe

Instagram: Richardrowe1876

Email: Richardroweministry@gmail.com